EXCITING
philippines
a visual journey

Welcome to the Philippines,
an Amazing Archipelago
of Enchanted Islands

PERIPLUS

EXCITING
philippines

a visual journey

THE PHILIPPINES is a Southeast Asian archipelago of over 7,000 islands strewn between the Pacific Ocean and the China Sea. Here Orient meets Occident with a distinctive flair. Three centuries of Spanish Christianization and 40 years of American colonization have left their mark, contributing to the East-West character of a volatile, Latinized people of Asian bloodlines. Catholicism is the major religion, English the tongue of the educated, and the soulful creativity of the Filipinos prevails in visual arts and handicraft. Music, basketball, boxing and politics are the national pastimes, from bustling Metro Manila to historical Cebu to booming Davao in Mindanao. Eco-tourism adventures await in the 79 provinces—from Boracay to Bohol, Panay to Palawan, to the Banaue Rice Terraces of Northern Luzon. All in this high-spirited place, the Philippines.

mabuhay!

WELCOME to one unique Filipino national sensibility—hospitality. Unlike any other Asian nation, the Philippines is a destination readily accessible to visitors from both East and West. Warmth and accommodation come naturally to the islander Filipinos. Guests are feted, honored and shown the best of the country's offerings.

The Philippines can be an exciting, even flamboyant place, driven by the exuberant spirit of the Filipino people. Their hybrid culture derives from a unique mingling of Eastern and Western influences, from diverse Malay, Chinese, Spanish and American strains and bloodlines. Their special character was formed by "four centuries in the convent and four decades in Hollywood," wrote historian Carmen Guerrero Nakpil. However one sees it, Filipinos have evolved a real cosmopolitan flair, topped by their national knack for song, dance and theater throughout seven regions. Welcome to the Philippine Islands' abundance of natural attractions and rich archipelagic experiences beyond the urban centers.

Below: Yellow daisy flower children, about to join the street parade at the Baguio Flower Festival in February.
Facing page: Life is a beach on Boracay, one of the top destinations in the Philippines.

Mabuhay is the *aloha* greeting of the Philippines. In one word, Mabuhay hails: welcome, farewell and long-live. Spirited Filipinos are the most hospitable people in the world.

Facing page: A Nayon Pilipino smile and a red *terno*, the Filipina's national costume.
Right: Cone-shaped Mt Mayon, the main attraction and active volcano of Bicol.
Middle, left: Fresh catch of the day, served on Isla Naburot, Iloilo.
Middle, right: Civic parade passing the heavyset Basilica of Taal, Batangas.
Bottom: Surfboards at sunset on the northern Ilocos coast of the big island, Luzon.

Over the centuries, both Spain and America have colonized this fragmented archipelago and left behind their traces—in staunch Roman Catholicism, the Spanish attitude of *manana* and the American-accented tongue and legislative system. Early Malay-Filipinos intermarried with Chinese and Arabs from the 10th century onwards and were colonized by the Spanish from the 16th to the 19th centuries. The Americans arrived in 1898 and occupied the islands for four decades. In 1946, after the devastation of World War II, the Philippines took its place as Asia's first constitutional democracy. In 1986 and 2001, two popular uprisings called People Power ousted bad leaders, renewed the sense of national self and installed the best Filipinos—women—as Presidents!

meet

Above: Manila wedding in grand style.

Right: Beauty and bougainvilleas on a footbridge in Davao.

Facing page, top left: Blue face paint on a brown-face windsurfer; it's just sunblock, the bathing costume of party island Boracay.

Facing page, top right: Exotic Davao beckons with a pretty face.

Facing page, bottom: Rice harvest in Bicol, under the gaze of Mt Mayon.

the filipinos

They are natural musicians and Westernized Asians—a combination
of dusky Malay and fiery Spanish, with a touch of Chinese and a
generous topping of hip, savvy America.

ILIPINOS are dancing-est folks with smiles, easy-
going characters and personal kinship systems that
keep their world going. Thespian Rolando Tinio
said it best: "Like islanders everywhere in the
tropics, Filipinos do tend to be quite blissful."
There are two sources of the inner strength and
friendliness of the typical Filipino: a fervent belief
in the goodness of God, Life and Nature, and a
sense of security in and reliance on family ties and
neighborhood associations. The typical Filipino is
long on religiosity, family, hometown loyalty and
cockeyed optimism.

STUDIES ON FILIPINO BEHAVIOR have pointed out distinct values and patterns in Filipino society: *pakikisama* or getting on well with associates; *utang na loob*, which means a deep sense of gratitude for favors received; *hiya* or a strong fear of losing face; and a *bahala na* attitude—things will take care of themselves. Filipinos live in a modern world without being thoroughly modern. The majority are people still in the bosom of Mother Nature—noble savages, both charming and exasperating.

Facing page: The jaunty jeepney driver in his psychedelic chimera of public transport is the macho man of Metro Manila.
Top: Smiling Davao girl with Mindanao dove.
Above: Proud Maranao women before a highborn household of Marawi City.
Right: Flamenco dance in front of the Philippine Senate.
Far right: Selling fresh *baco* juice at the Carbon Market in Cebu.

a bastion of

christianity

Centuries of Spanish colonization and a native love of harvest rituals have left the country with "earthquake baroque" stone churches and a bounty of colorful fiestas.

The PHILIPPINES is the only predominantly Christian nation in Asia. Eighty percent Roman Catholic and traditionally pious, Filipinos live in a world of parish priests, nuns, cardinals and patron saints who are revered in households through painted wooden *santos*. The Virgin Mary (called Mama Mary) is the standard bearer of Filipino Catholicism around Luzon, while the Santo Nino (the Child Jesus), in ermine cloak and golden crown, is everyone's favorite holy babe in the Visayas.

Facing page: Baguio's pink cathedral has risen again from the ashes of the 1990 Luzon earthquake.
Top: Lone padre walks the halls of ancient San Augustin Church in Intramuros.
Below: The Moriones Festival portrays Christ's crucifixion among Roman legionnaires.

THE LEGACY of three centuries of Spanish colonization manifests itself among the oldest Catholic
churches of the country. From ancient San Agustin
Church with its carved doors and Chinese *fu* lions
to fine painted ceilings in medieval Intramuros to
Ilocandia up north, where the heavyset "earthquake
baroque" churches of Paoay, Santa Maria and Santa
Lucia stand.

While the family kinship system binds together
the country's 79 provinces, it is Catholicism, the
common religion and social glue, that underlines
the lifestyle—especially at fiesta time. Secular harvest
feasts merge with Christian worship as in the Feast of
the Santo Nino, and the Visayans celebrate dancing
fiestas such as the Ati-Atihan of Kalibo, Sinugba of
Cebu and Dinagyang of Iloilo. During Eastertime or
Holy Week, the island of Marinduque presents the
dramatic spectacle of the Moriones Festival,
reenacting the miraculous conversion of the Biblical
legionnaire Longinus. Quezon's Pahiyas or "Harvest
Offering" honors San Isidro de Labrador, patron saint
of farmers; homes are decorated with fruits of the
harvest and colored rice wafers called *kiping*.

Facing page: Mother Mary
prays for us near the Bantay
belltower of Vigan.
Left: Magellan's Cross planted
Catholicism in the center of
Cebu in 1517.
Middle, left: Blessed is the
sleeping babe among the
Mama Marys and Santo Ninos.
Middle, right: Lighting votive
candles in Baclaran Redempt-
orist Church on Wednesdays.
Bottom, left: Candlelit pro-
cession of "La Naval" from
Santo Domingo Church in
Quezon City.
Bottom, right: Stark and spare
San Joaquin Church in isolated
Batanes, northernmost islands
of the Philippines.

manila by the bay

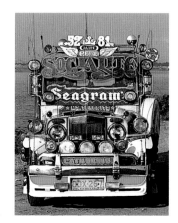

Manila began along the banks of the Pasig River, within Intramuros, the medieval Walled City. Today some twelve million urbanites jostle through Metro Manila, a chaotic, modern Asian metropolis.

To TOUCH THE HEART of old Manila, start with Rizal Park, Intramuros and Fort Santiago on the Pasig River—guardpost of the Spanish Walled City for three centuries. This medieval fortress with high walls contained the temporal and spiritual worlds, but few traces remain today beyond the stony gates. Visit the museums where Intramuros' memories are kept: Casa Manila near ancient San Agustin Church and the new Bahay Tsinoy (Chinese-Filipino) Museum. The creativity of the Filipinos is showcased in the Metropolitan Museum of Art, Coconut Palace and Cultural Center of the Philippines by the bayside.

Facing page, top: The chimera of public transportation, the colorful jeepney, can be found everywhere.
Facing page, bottom: Ayala Avenue, showing Makati's sleek, soaring cityscape.
Clockwise from top right: Sunset over the Ayala Center, commercial and residential heart of Makati. A corner *baluarte* (balustraded fort), intact among the adobe walls of medieval Intramuros. Saling Pusa, young artists of Antipolo, by the big Jeepney Mural of Luneta. The EDSA highway crossing Ortigas, civic heart of Manila, marked by the giant EDSA Shrine.

MANILA'S ONLY HIGHRISE AREA is Makati, the modern satellite hub of big business, new ideas and progress. In Makati are classy hotels, upscale malls and East-West fusion cuisine restaurants; the financial district (Ayala Avenue); and elite residential villages. Everything is bigger, brighter and shinier in Makati, the new millennium side of Metro Manila.

Manila's big, circumferential highway is known affectionately as EDSA and has carried miraculous popular uprisings called "People Power." Together with the new Metro Railway Transit, EDSA links the

Clockwise from top: Manila's oldest church, San Augustin, has trompe l'oeil inside and a coral facelift outside.
Calesa rides and cobblestones spell nostalgia near Casa Manila, Intramuros.
Good Luck Ice Cream licks the Manila heat wherever there are kids around.
Rizal Park by the bay with its flags, where Manila begins at kilometer 0.

Facing page, clockwise:
The famous Manila Bay sunset.
Corregidor Island can be reached from Manila by hydrofoil. "The Rock" was made famous by the Allies' defence in 1942. Corregidor with its military installations and delightful scenery is a popular day-trip.
The gateway to Fort Santiago, the military outpost guarding Manila for three centuries.

major city hubs: Roxas Boulevard, rimming Manila Bay to Makati with her spiffy Ayala Center; Ortigas Center in Pasig, where mega-sized shopping malls drive the consumer spirit; and Cubao in middle-class Quezon City, with its mass entertainment, music clubs and big university population.

Manila's urban sprawl is interknit by a massive case of Asian traffic—and colorful jeepneys. The virtual icon of Manila is the ubiquitous jeepney, that colorful chimera of public transportation that plies the city byways on short, zippy hauls. These multipassenger vehicles hark back to the days of American GI jeeps, even while they carry the cityfolk forward—with machismo—into the 21st century.

A popular escape from the madding crowd (and tourists' war memorial tour) is a foray to the Rock of Corregidor, the fortified island guarding Manila Bay. The Rock was the Allies' last bastion in the Pacific War. Today, visitors pay respects to the WW II gun battlements and underground tunnels where Filipino and American soldiers shared courage and history.

After the famous orange sunset on Manila Bay, night scenes light up the new yuppie entertainment area of Malate, behind the austere old Resurrection Church. Malate today means urban renewal on a charming scale: lots of stylish cosmopolitan cafés and crafts galleries cluster around Remedios Circle—like fireflies amid the night and music.

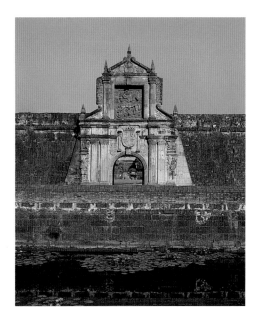

tagaytay
&
cavite

Taal Volcano within a scenic lake is a popular attraction outside Manila. The vantage point is Tagaytay—Cavite's resort town high on the ridge above the lakeshore.

Facing page, top: Tagaytay Ridge always means spectacular lakeviews and native pony rides.

Facing page, bottom: Serene Taal Lake at sunset belies the smallest, most treacherous volcano in the land.

Right: Kawit, Cavite, home of General Emilio Aguinaldo, first President of the Republic.

Middle, left: Tagaytay means fruits and more fruits—here marketed with a lakeview.

Middle, right: General Aguinaldo designed this remarkable mansion himself.

Bottom: The crater lake of Taal Volcano within Taal Lake in Batangas Province.

TAGAYTAY IS KNOWN for fruit stalls, horseback rides, spectacular scenery, cool climes and sunrises over Taal Lake. From this viewpoint 700 m up, one gazes upon the world's smallest, lowest volcano—a peaceful island-within-a-lake-within-an-island. Culture seekers drive to Cavite—the "Province of Heroes"—to remember their revolutionary forbears. In Kawit stands the historic home of General Emilio Aguinaldo, first President of the Republic in 1896 and soldier, strategist and architect. In Las Pinas resides the famous Bamboo Organ, centerpiece of a February concert festival. In Dasmarinas, the new De La Salle Museum displays the Filipinos' grand traditional lifestyle.

laguna & calabarzon

Just outside Manila lie five Tagalog provinces where one feels the pastoral rhythms of the country. "Calabarzon" encompasses Cavite, Laguna, Batangas, Rizal and Quezon.

Laguna is a riverine province with a heart-shaped lake. Life here is cooler, wetter, more languorous. Rural forays will let you experience warm hospitality, local delicacies and the joys of rivers and springs. Refresh in the bubbly pools of Hidden Valley Springs. Ride the famous rapids of Pagsanjan River. Enjoy Villa Escudero on the border—a coconut plantation-cum-resort that offers day-trips to costumed nostalgia and watery picnics. Visit Taal, Batangas, with her huge basilica, see *balisong* knives and historic houses. Lucban and Sariaya towns in Quezon celebrate the charming Pahiyas Festival, when farmers decorate their homes with the harvest—fruit, vegetables and colored rice wafers called *kiping*.

Facing page, top: Waters from Villa Escudero's waterfall run through the picnic area.
Facing page, bottom: The Villa's cottages by the water —the coconut hacienda's own river.

Clockwise from top left: Pagsanjan's Shoot-the-Rapids ride is a memorable trip for visitors! Novel "Carabator" or carabao-drawn wagon tours the Villa's haciendas. Another weekenders' resort is popular Matabunkay Beach, Batangas. Pagsanjan River's source is the Magdapio waterfall, under which you will love to go rafting. Pahiyas Fiesta of Lucban, Quezon; homes are decorated with *kiping*.

watersports from

batangas to bohol

The Philippines has 43,000 sq km of coral reefs and a great diversity of marine life for the sports diver. The archipelago's long, balmy coastlines are ideal for boating, windsurfing, kayaking and swimming.

WEEKENDING BY THE SEA often means going to Matabunkay, Nasugbu or Anilao, three sunny spots on the western shore of Batangas. The climate runs hot, the hills are rugged (like its people), and cityfolk head for the coastlines for scuba diving of all levels. Puerto Galera is on Mindoro Island, an hour's ferry ride across the straits from Batangas City. There are 13 beaches developed around picturesque PG, 25 excellent dive sites and facilities for camping, fishing, boating, tennis, golf, as well as nightlife. Bohol also harbors memorable diving sites round the smaller isles of Panglao and Balicasag.

Facing page, top: Outrigger *banca* beached on a white shoreline of Bohol Island. **Left:** Lavender sunset falls over rustic Coco Beach Resort in Puerto Galera. **Below:** White sands and crystal waters of Pamalican Island, site of the exclusive Amanpulo Resort.

Clockwise from top left:
Snorkeling in the clear waters of Hundred Islands, Pangasinan. The Bali Hai Resort in Bauang, La Union, on the west coast of Luzon. Taking scuba diving instruction at Dakak Resort, Dapitan, Zamboanga. Fishing near the Amanpulo Resort. Marine coral reefs from Batangas to Bohol offer seductive diving year-round. Guests' fleet of colorful sailing boats at Dakak Resort.
Facing page: Windsurfing by a beach resort off the coast of Argao, Cebu.

vigan &
ilocandia

Ilocandia is a sparse and rugged land. Three northwestern provinces hug the northern coastline of Luzon—between the mountains and the sea—and harbor the cultural treasure known as Vigan.

Facing page: Old streets of Heritage village in Vigan; the tall stone mansions date back to 17th-century Chinese merchants.
Above: Boys and their goat in the warm Ilocos sunset.
Below: Paoay Church in Ilocos Sur is supported by thick stone buttresses—a unique style called "earthquake baroque."

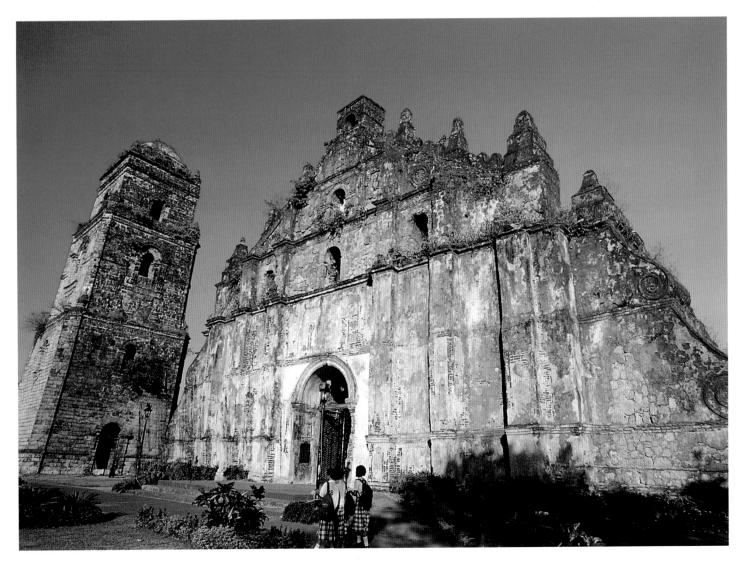

Clockwise from left: A boy of Ilocos sells Vigan souvenir cowboy hats made of woven bamboo. Vigan's traditional *burnayan* or pottery kiln makes pots in a giant wood-fired oven. *Molave* benches and old sugar mills on the sidewalk—part of the town's reproduction furniture trade. Venture northward and explore the cultural history museum of Laoag, Ilocos Norte. Cobbled streets among Vigan houses are a playground for kids with wheels.

ILOCANDIA IS A RUGGED LAND comprising the northwestern provinces of La Union, Ilocos Sur and Norte where fields of tobacco, lone fishermen on dunelike shores and the finest highways of Luzon give Ilocandia a sparse, spare beauty. Vigan in Ilocos Sur is a heritage village stuck in time. It exudes an austere antiquity, especially the towering 18th-century mansions, all lined along cobblestone streets running straight and narrow between quarters. Visitors can view the elegant Quema mansion or stay in Villa Angela Heritage House, with its polished wooden floors, capiz windows and charm galore, or tarry at the old *burnayan*, the traditional pottery kiln.

Above, left: Old iron bridge over troubled waters, a land-mark of hardy Ilocandia.
Above, right: Jesus Christ as a wood carving, on one of the streets of Vigan, Ilocos Sur.
Left: A low-slung *carretela* (horse carriage) of Vigan parks by the Bantay belltower.

Above: The Banaue rice terraces were hand-built by the Ifugaos over 2,000 years ago.
Facing page, top and bottom: Treks around Ifugao and Bontoc expose visitors to the awesome sights of the highland.
Five major tribal groups collectively known as Igorots live in the Cordillera.

baguio &

THE BANAUE RICE TERRACES in the Cordillera are the scenic highlight of Luzon. The grandeur of the rice terraces, along with the traditional lifestyle of the Ifugao tribespeople, make for a unique experience in the highlands. It's a hiker's mecca too. Ascend to the top and see the 100-sq-km range of terraces, carved by hand over 2,000 years ago. Wander Banaue town, or trek to Batad. Explore Sagada, the episcopal mission town in Bontoc, where coffins hang in great caves and massive limestone rocks mark the pathways. The awesome landscapes and ethnic traditions of the Cordillera create long-lasting impressions.

the cordillera

Behold the Banaue Rice Terraces and the hardy lifestyle of the Ifugao tribespeople for a unique experience of the Cordillera highlands.

bAGUIO CITY, the highland summer capital first established by the Americans in 1902, promises a springtime climate (20°C) and pine trees at 1,500 m above sea level. Baguio also means: a cowboy spirit among the cityfolk; horseback rides for tourists and evergreen attractions such as rollerskating and boating in Burnham Park; fresh strawberry jam and pink nuns. Baguio has the most colorful public market in the country—hanging with baskets, fruits, vegetables and golden, "everlasting" garlands. Baguio spells: schools and churches; golf courses and gardens; old-mine tours, cafés with fresh bread and serious coffee; plus a bazaar of souvenirs in silver and wood. The newest attraction is Tam-Awan, a recreated village of Igorot houses with art exhibits by indigenous artists.

Clockwise from left: Ifugao hut made of hardwood and thatch, in Tam-Awan Village, Baguio. The Flower Festival brings out the Kalinga costumes and Baguio beauties. Pony boys and horses in the morning mist of Wright Park in Baguio. Baguio has nurtured modern artwork from a guild of indigenous artists. Planting upland rice in a watery plot of Banaue in the Cordillera. Baguio's Burnham Park is a family place for leisure boating and biking.
Facing page: Just another day harvesting rice on the high stone terraces of Ifugao.

cebu & the visayan isles

Hanging midway down the archipelago like a necklace of uneven pearls, the Visayas comprise six major islands —Cebu, Bohol, Negros, Panay, Leyte and Samar—and their fringe isles.

Facing page, top: Beach bunny in bikini on Mactan, Cebu's own resorts isle.
Facing page, bottom: The tropical resort formula: white sandy beach, aqua sea, palm trees and picturesque cottages —here those of Argao, Cebu.
Top: Cebu by night means food, entertainment and city traffic.
Left: Basilica of Santo Nino in Cebu with the Sinulog parade.

VIVE LA DIFFERENCE of the Visayas: the slower pace of life; the seductive lilt of the languages; the loving women; the seafood, beaches, guitars; and the sweetest of mangoes. Cebu—Queen City of the South—was recently named the eighth most livable city in Asia! The Cebuanos work harder, try harder and have created the second biggest city in the country. Cebu boasts an international airport and malls and convention centers within this historical cradle of 16th-century Spanish Philippines.

bUSINESS-MINDED CEBU is a manufacturing center and port, doing a thriving trade in handicrafts and accessories, furniture and guitars. Taste the seafood. Enjoy the nightlife. See Magellan's Cross, the Basilica of the Santo Nino, and Casa Gorordo for a glimpse of the city's heritage. Catch Sinulog, Cebu's dancing, costumed parade in January.

Iloilo possesses the gentility of a bygone era, with its lovely ancestral houses of the Jaro district, the folksy carvings on Iloilo's old churches and some of the nicest people and pastries of the Visayas! For adventure seekers, there's exotic Isla Naburot, a private isle southwest of Guimaras Island. From Iloilo, take a ferry to Bacolod in Negros, island of the sugar barons and golfing center of the Visayas. Here the Negrense people live hard, play hard and enjoy the lifestyle of the modern *haciendero*. Both creative crafts and wild notions originate here. Visit Silay town to the north, with its ancestral mansions and orchid farms. And be in Bacolod when the stunning Masskara Festival unravels on the streets.

For scuba diving, plunge into the seas of Bohol, southeast of Cebu, where rich fishing waters flow over some of the Philippines' most seductive dive sites.

Facing page: Isla Naburot, off Guimaras and Iloilo, is a private isle made for adventurous, Robinson Crusoe-type guests.
Top, left: A resort cottage right by the sea, for holiday-makers in southern Cebu.
Top, right: Masskara is a thanksgiving and Mardi Gras—the ultimate costumed revelry of Bacolod, Negros Oriental.
Above: This is Plantation Bay Hotel on Mactan Island, a far-out fantasy resort built round a shallow lagoon.
Left: Guitars are a specialized product from craftsy, musical Cebu.

boracay

Boracay, an island of white, flourlike sands and crystal-clear waters, has been named one of the best beaches in the world.

Facing page: Boracay has sleek *bancas* for island-hopping and photo opportunities everywhere.
Top: Peace and solitude and a shady hut on the wide, white Boracay shore.
Middle: Sunshine, surfboards and a long tropical drink make the holiday.
Right: Boracay is considered the windsurfing capital of the Philippines.

bORACAY, OFF AKLAN PROVINCE, is one long (7 km) beautiful white beach, regarded as one of the best beaches in the world, though it is lined by a hundred resorts—from long-stay budget rooms to high-end quarters in paradise. Beach culture has covered the entire island; today, 6,000 Boracay residents entertain some two million tourists a year. Both locals and foreigners flock to this faraway isle, for it is an exceptional confluence of pure, white flourlike sands and crystal-clear waters that ripple in the sun before turning turquoise over the depths. Boracay is one of the most enduring traveler's meccas.

Top, left: Boracay T-shirts explode in the wild colors of the beach holiday.
Top, right: Sunset cocktails by the pool with jazz music, before Boracay's disco night takes over.
Middle, left: A golf course has arrived on Boracay.
Middle, right: Beach, beach and more beach.
Left: Sea kayaking, a meditative activity with the sea, has joined the resort isle's roster of waterborne sports.
Facing page: Fine white beach, golden girl and coconut palms in the breeze.

the palawan archipelago

Palawan, especially its northern islands, soars with dramatic landscapes of granite and limestone, great caves and pristine beaches. Underwater, she astounds with marine landscapes that inspire superlatives from divers and environmentalists.

Facing page: Yellow kayak adrift in Coron's green lagoon.
Right: Charter planes and silver jeepneys ferry guests to Northern Palawan resorts.
Below, left: Big, white *banca* runs island explorers around fascinating Bacuit Bay.
Below, right: Snorkeling in the Big Lagoon near El Nido Resort, Miniloc Island.

Palawan is a long, exciting archipelago of 1,700 islands, stretching 553 km southwest of Manila and leaning close to Borneo in terms of geography and geology. Here is 400 km of land comprising the last frontier—both for island adventurers and an exotic array of endemic wildlife species. The capital, Puerto Princesa, has been named the cleanest town in the country, and hailed as the gateway to the natural wonders of the Palawan frontier. Northward, you will find St Paul's Underground River, Palawan's wonder-of-the-natural-world attraction. Far southward are the Tabon Caves, a tribal area where the remains of early man have been discovered. Due east, in the midst of the Sulu Sea, lie the diving waters scuba fans rave about: Tubbataha Reef.

hEAD TO NORTHERN PALAWAN for more exotic discoveries. Bacuit Bay abounds with spectacular nature spots, cathedral caves, marine gardens, black granite cliffs and pristine white sand beaches. All around soar dramatic landscapes of limestone, as well as unique marine seascapes.

Beyond the wonders of Nature, numerous chic boutique resorts have sprouted in the farthest reaches of Palawan. There are the El Nido Resorts, providing glamorous accommodations on stilts. Off sprawling Busuanga, there's Club Paradise, a favorite destination among expats, while nearby Calauit Nature Park harbors a selection of African savannah animals. Ensconced on the farthest outpost of Cuyo is Amanpulo, the boutique resort that is an icon of superstar luxury.

Facing page, clockwise from left: Pristine sands and crystal waters of the Cuyo Islands, site of Amanpulo. Calauit Island's Nature Park is home to giraffes, zebras and other African species. El Nido spells limestone caves cliffs and monoliths where gatherers climb to collect birds' nests for gourmet cuisine.

Clockwise from right: Club Noah-Isabelle in Taytay features cottages on stilts over water. Amanpulo's luxury casitas afford guests ultimate comfort and privacy. Coron Bay near Busuanga inspires fantastic sunsets and nature trips on land and water. Monkey walks the fiery Palawan sunset; the frontier land is wild and wondrous.

mindanao
—island of adventure

Mindanao, the largest island of the Southern Philippines, belongs to adventure travelers. Teeming with natural resources (along with a reputation for turbulence), Mindanao offers a tapestry of sights and experiences, from exotic flora and fauna to the fascinating cultures of tribal minorities.

MINDANAO, THE GREAT ISLAND south of the Visayas, is the Philippines' pioneer land, offering myriad experiences far from the madding urban crowd. Far-off Zamboanga on the northern edge of the Sulu Sea is the melting pot of the south, with five tribal minority groups coloring the cosmopolitan port town. Visitors can see the Muslim-influenced architecture of the Tausug, Yakan and Subanon among the churches, parks and botanical gardens. Just offshore, the stilt villages and boats of the Samal-Badjao people lend an exotic cachet, as Zamboanga sails onward under the image of sea gypsies' *vintas*—outrigger boats with multi-colored sails.

Facing page, top: Davao Mandaya family in tribal costumes.
Facing page, bottom: Volcanic Mt Hibok-Hibok as seen from the White Island of Camiguin.
Top: Zamboanga girl on a colorful *vinta* of the Sulu Seas.
Middle, left: Aerial view of Dakak Resort, Zamboanga del Norte.
Middle, right: Giant tuna harvest in General Santos, fishing port of Southern Mindanao.
Right: Clouds and mystery hover around Camiguin, an island of seven volcanoes.

Right: A clown face among the festive fruits of Davao's Kadayawan Fiesta.
Below: A Mandaya weaver produces hemp cloth called *dagmay* on a backstrap loom.
Facing page, top to bottom: The Kadayawan Festival brings out the exotic costumes of the regional tribes. Davao's Apo View Hotel looks out over rolling golf links. Picturesque three-tiered gazebo and Samal-style cottages at the Pearl Farm.

MINDANAO for the tourist often means Davao, the thriving industrial hub and province on the southeast quadrant. Davao City, one of the most expansive cities in the world, is big on exotic fruits, big on seafood and fish (exported through the port of General Santos), and big of heart for endangered species: in the foothills of Mt Apo (the country's highest peak) the Eagle Center breeds the endangered national bird, the Philippine Eagle. Davao is a sensual experience of orchid blooms (such as the vibrant *waling-waling*) and inimitable

durians; of religious shrines and mountain climbing to the country's highest peak; of exotic fruit such as *marang*, mangosteen, rambutan and *lanzones*; and of *abaca* hemp weavings called *dagmay*, loomed by the Mandayan tribespeople for tie-dyed, earth-toned clothing and home decor. Davao is also the home of the Kadayawan Festival, when the highly decorative tribes of T'bolis and Bagobos converge and celebrate.

Mindanao welcomes sun and beach lovers. For some, the picturesque designer resort Pearl Farm on Samal Island south of Davao is reason enough for venturing to Mindanao. The luckiest adventure travelers have discovered Siargao town off Surigao for its surfing and scenery, and Camiguin Island off Cagayan de Oro for its natural hot and cold springs and many volcanic splendors. Tiny, tear-shaped Camiguin is an exceptionally beautiful isle of seven volcanoes amid forested hills, rimmed by rolling white sand beaches.

Plentiful natural materials and the innate "soulful creativity" of the Filipinos make the Philippines a treasure trove for crafts.

local crafts

EVERY REGION of the archipelago is a delightful source of small, handmade souvenirs, basketry and home decor made from shells, paper, resin, wood or ethnic fabric. Crafts made from natural materials run from charming (for the tourist) to sublime (for the collector)—from the *jusi* silk of the *barong tagalog* (national shirt) to a bright shawl of Philippine silk; from sheer *pina* (from the wild pineapple plant) to the rustic *abaca* or *raffia* palms in table placemats. Be it baskets, backpacks, wood carvings or fabrics; the finest wood carvings from Ifugao; unique shell-craft combining capiz or mother-of-pearl with wood or metal—you can find these handicrafts at the best handicraft centres in Manila, such as Silahis Crafts in Intramuros, Tesoros in Ermita or Makati, and the Filipiniana sections of large stores.

Facing page, top: Filipino masks like these are sold in tourist markets.

Facing page, bottom: Visayan women plait fine pandan leaves into decorative sleeping mats.

Top, left to right: Townsfolk of Balisong, Batangas, handcrafting the dazzling "butterfly knives." Paper-mâché horses for sale in Angono, Rizal. Woven mat.

Middle, left and right: Etched Moro gongs and a large kris on a *kulintang* (xylophone); these are the metal crafts of the Muslims of Mindanao. Filipino baskets—a popular souvenir.

Left: A Mandaya girl of Davao with a weaving loom strapped across her back.

filipino food

Filipino food is a blend of Malay, Spanish and Chinese influences. Seafood, chicken and pork come in sauces of garlic, vinegar, soy, calamansi and coconut.

K *AIN-NA!* LET'S EAT! A typical Filipino family meal begins with a variety of tropical fish and crustaceans and continues through a melange of basic spices—garlic, ginger, vinegar, soy sauce and calamansi (sweet baby limes). Seafood, chicken and pork are sautéed, stewed or roasted as main courses, while desserts are concocted with coconut milk, rice flour, sugar and lots of tropical fruits.

Facing page: A posh seafood buffet is served up from Bacolod's seas.
Above: A big tropical fruit spread in a *banca* at the Costa Aguada Resort.
Left: An array of Filipino desserts on a banana leaf—rice patties with sesame and coconut, *Palitao* (left), brown rice cake, *Kutsinta* (middle) and cassava patties with coconut, *Pichi-Pichi* (right).

Right: Roast fish barbecue and coconut bowls make for a chic beach picnic in Palawan.
Below: More smiles and fresh seafood at sunset.
Facing page, clockwise: *Lechon* does a thriving business during celebrations. *Longganisa* are pork sausages, a specialty of select provinces. Fresh lobsters with a tranquil seaview of Samal Island. Exotic tropical fruits such as mangoes, durian and starfruit are exported from Cebu.

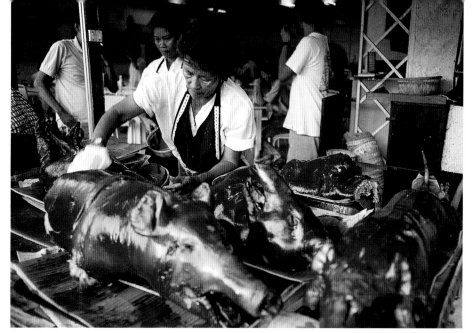

HE *LECHON* or roast suckling pig—centerpiece of a Filipino fiesta—is roasted over coals till it's golden crispy and served with a sweet liver sauce. *Sinigang* is the local bouillabaisse, containing seafood or meat cooked in a mildly sour broth. *Adobo* is a popular chicken or pork dish, stewed with soy sauce, vinegar, garlic and peppercorns. Filipinos are blessed with an exotic variety of tropical fruit—from the incomparable Philippine mango to myriad bananas, pineapples, *atis, chico*, durian and mangosteen. Traveling foodies should also watch out for the varied regional cuisines offered at hotel buffets—especially the rich and tasty cooking from Pampanga, province of the best cooks.

music & dance

Whether artist or artiste, folksy or fine, Filipinos are artful performers of unique caliber. In music, song and dance, they excel in Asia.

IN THE PERFORMING ARTS, the Filipino is a sheer adept and cultural accumulator. Especially in Western pop music: what was once local musicians' imitation of the American country-western sound has evolved into a movable feast of original Filipino music. Filipino bands now roam the nightclubs and hotels of Asia, and individual musicians have become the most versatile singing icons and serenaders of Asia, in three languages. Top billed pop performers such as Kuh Ledesma, Regine Velasquez and Gary Valenciano (with his superb dancing form) turn out rave musical productions unparalleled in the region.

Filipinos excel in dancing—on stage or on the street. Cities have their own ballet schools, folk dance groups and show troupes for television, promotions and special events. And of course, there is the public theater of the streets, unraveling in every town fiesta filled with costumed dancing parades.

Filipinos love everything showbiz and entertainment—it comes merged with American pop and national politics. Legitimate theater is alive and well in Manila's theater companies such as Repertory Philippines, based at Shaw Center, Ortigas, and the Filipino-language drama of the main theater of the Cultural Center. There is also Trumpets Playhouse and New Voice Theater for children's musicals and women's drama.

Facing page, top: Muslim dancer on an ancient wall.
Facing page, bottom: Feminine "flowers" dancing in Baguio's own Flower Festival in February.
Below: "Singkil" with fans, performed by a Bayanihan folk dancer.
Bottom: Typical Filipino band hangs out in their Quezon City music club.

dANCE has also emerged as a fine art form. Several companies—Ballet Philippines, Philippine Ballet Theater and Ballet Manila—perform classical repertoires each season. Then there's BP's modern dance event, the "Neo Filipino Series," which has been in performance for eight innovative years, presenting collaborations between the avant-garde and the classical arts, harnessing new music and video, as well as productions by creative designers. Neo-Filipino dance artistes with their stunning theaterpieces have been called counterpoint choreographers and sophisticated rebels.

Facing page, clockwise from top left: Bayanihan folk dancers make ready for the rural hat dance. A costumed Cebuana carries her Santo Nino in the Sinulog Festival. Grace Nono, small but stunning ethnic rock priestess, and the Pinikpikan band.

Clockwise from top left: Elder's own revelry in the pagan-Christian fusion of the Ati-Atihan Fiesta. "Roman soldier" taking a music break from the Moriones Festival of Marinduque. Ballet Philippines dance troupe on an outreach tour from the Cultural Center. The Ati-Atihan of Kalibo, Aklan, spawned a "generic" dance that is now performed everywhere.

All roads lead through Manila, gateway to the islands. Holidays begin when Filipinos—displaying their famous hospitality—greet you with friendly smiles and hip English.

visiting the philippines

THE BEST TIME to visit the Philippines is from mid-October through February—after the rains, but before the hot summer months of April and May. The four festive months comprise the best time for beachgoing and touring; and January is a good time to catch the Visayas' dancing fiestas. Most visitors come to Manila by air, arriving at Ninoy Aquino International Airport or Cebu's Mactan International Airport (30 minutes from the beach). With some planning, one can spend a varied week on these shores, going on a city tour of Intramuros, Fort Santiago and Manila's new cultural museums; on day-trips to Pagsanjan Falls, Villa Escudero or Tagaytay Ridge; or island-hopping down to the resort beaches of Cebu or Boracay.

Facing page, top: Flower children at the Pahiyas Festival in Lucban, Quezon.
Facing page, bottom: Swimming pool and open thatched restaurant of the China Sea Resort in Bauang, La Union, on the West Coast of Luzon.
Clockwise from top: Swimming pool of the Mayon International Hotel in Legaspi City, with Mayon Volcano looming in the background. The Costa Aguada Resort on Guimaras spells provincial pleasures for families. Amanpulo resort casita on Cuyo Island stands for six-star luxury in the utmost privacy. Mountain bikes for an island-hopping excursion, Boracay.

Front cover, top to bottom:
Baguio Cathedral. Filipina in
a red *terno*, the national
costume. Catamaran and
Boracay beach.
Back cover, top to bottom:
Manila cityscape at night. Girl
presenting a basket of shells
on Santa Cruz Island. Banaue
rice terraces. Manila jeepney.
Front endpaper: Sunset
beach stroll.

Published by Periplus Editions (HK) Ltd

Copyright © 2001 Periplus Editions (HK) Ltd

ISBN 962-593-745-5

Distributors:

Asia Pacific
Berkeley Books Pte Ltd
5 Little Road, #08-01
Singapore 536983
Tel: (65) 280-1330
Fax: (65) 280-6290

Japan and Korea
Tuttle Publishing
RK Building, 2nd Floor
2-13-10 Shimo-Meguro
Meguro-ku, Tokyo 153-0064
Tel: (03) 5437-0171
Fax: (03) 5437-0755

USA, Canada, UK, Europe
Tuttle Publishing
Distribution Center
Airport Industrial Park
364 Innovation Drive
North Clarendon, VT 05759-9436
Tel: (802) 773-8930
Fax: (800) 526-2778

Publisher: Eric M. Oey
Writer: Elizabeth V. Reyes
Editor: Michael Stachels

Printed in Singapore

Photographic Credits

Beck, Joseph (Photobank Singapore), back cover (bottom), pp. 5 (top), 45 (bottom left).
Beiboer, Paul, p. 35 (middle left).
Bautista, Bien S., pp. 4, 7 (middle right), 8 (bottom), 13 (top), 14, 15 (top), 16 (top), 17 (top left), 19 (top), 20 (top), 21 (middle left), 23 (top left, middle left, middle right and bottom), 24 (bottom), 34, 35 (top left, top right and bottom right), 39 (middle right), 46 (left and top right), 47 (top left), 49 (middle right), 52, 53 (top center and middle right), 59 (bottom), 61 (bottom).
Davocol, Emil V., front cover (top right and bottom), back cover (top), front endpaper, pp. 1, 2, 7 (bottom), 10, 11 (top), 12, 16 (bottom), 17 (top right), 18 (top, middle left and middle right), 22 (bottom), 24 (top), 26 (bottom left), 27, 28, 29, 30 (top left, middle right and bottom left), 31 (top left and bottom), 32, 33 (bottom), 35 (middle right), 36 (bottom), 37 (top), 39 (top right), 41 (top and bottom), 42 (middle right), 48 (top), 49 (middle left), 50, 51 (top and bottom), 53 (top left and bottom), 54, 57 (top left and top right), 58 (bottom), 62 (top).
Garbutt, Veronica, pp. 15 (bottom right), 19 (bottom right), 22 (top), 23 (top right), 26 (top right, middle left and middle right), 46 (bottom right), 55 (top), 57 (bottom left and bottom right), 62 (bottom), 63 (top).
Heaton, Dallas & John (Photobank Singapore), p. 39 (top left).
Jezierski, Ingo, pp. 36 (top), 64.
Lucero, Patrick Nasgaishi, back cover (middle left), pp. 7 (top and middle left), 9, 11 (middle right and bottom), 13 (bottom), 15 (middle left, middle right and bottom left), 18 (bottom), 25 (top), 26 (top left and bottom right), 30 (top right and bottom right), 31 (top right), 33 (top), 35 (bottom left), 37 (bottom), 39 (bottom), 41 (middle), 42 (top left, top right, middle left and bottom), 45 (top and bottom right), 47 (top right and bottom), 48 (bottom), 49 (top), 51 (middle), 53 (middle left), 56 (bottom), 60 (top right), 61 (top left, top right and middle right), 63 (top left and bottom left).
Montifar, Raul M., p. 44.
Simmons, Ben (Photobank Singapore), p. 11 (middle left).
Tettoni, Luca Invernizzi (Photobank Singapore), pp. 8 (top), 17 (bottom left and bottom right), 21 (top and middle right), 38, 47 (middle right), 53 (top right), 55 (bottom), 56 (top), 59 (top), 60 (top left and bottom).
Vidler, Steve (Photobank Singapore), front cover (top left), pp. 5 (bottom), 6, 19 (bottom left), 40, 43.
Wassman, Bill (Photobank Singapore), p. 58 (top).
Yabao, Sonny, back cover (middle right), pp. 20 (bottom), 21 (bottom), 49 (bottom right), 63 (bottom right).

Discover
exciting asia

Discover Asia with the *Exciting Asia* series. Each title is a visual guide to a different Asian destination. The stunning images within provide a fascinating introduction to each unique and special place. Learn about the country's people and lifestyle, their art and their culture.

New

Exciting India

text by Bikram Grewal
photography by Henry Wilson, Aditya Patankar and Kamal Sahai

India is a country of fascinating contrasts and an ancient civilization, the birthplace of Hinduism and Buddhism. This exciting pictorial takes you from the mighty Himalayas to the shore temples on the southern coasts.

ISBN 962 593 852 4
96 pages Hardcover
Publication: August 2001

Periplus Editions
Each Book: 225 x 300mm
US$16.95 Hardcover
US$9.95 Paperback

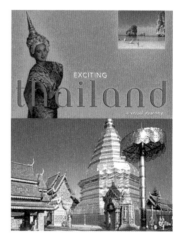

Exciting Bali

text by Patrick R. Booz
photography by Ian Lloyd

An unforgettable insight into the lush Indonesian "Island of the Gods".

ISBN 962 593 210 0
64 pages Paperback

Exciting Malaysia

text by S.L. Wong
photography by Arthur Teng, et al

A visual journey around a fascinating and diverse Southeast Asian nation.

ISBN 962 593 755 2
48 pages Hardcover

Exciting Singapore

text by David Blocksidge
photography by Ingo Jezierski, et al

Feast your eyes on the attractions of this prosperous island-republic.

ISBN 962 593 207 0
64 pages Hardcover

Exciting Thailand

text by Andrew Forbes
photography by Luca Invernizzi Tettoni

An amazing encounter with Thailand's remarkable people and places.

ISBN 962 593 211 9
64 pages Hardcover